Motif A

Afghans not only keep you warm and cozy they are also a great way to spruce up your décor. With five different styles to choose from you are sure to find one that will fit your needs, plus they are a perfect take along project.

LEISURE ARTS, INC. • Little Rock, Arkansas

Sunburst Hexagon Granny

 **EASY**

SHOPPING LIST

Yarn Worsted weight 🧶 **4** MEDIUM
yarn, 100% acrylic, [3½ oz /100g
(approx 170 yds / 156m)]
- ☐ Color A: 4 Skeins White
- ☐ Color B: 1 Skein Eggplant
- ☐ Color C: 1 Skein Dusty Rose
- ☐ Color D: 1 Skein Silver Blue
- ☐ Color E: 1 Skein Rose
- ☐ Color F: 1 Skein Dusty Green
- ☐ Color G: 1 Skein Fern
- ☐ Color H: 1 Skein Aqua
- ☐ Color I: 1 Skein Terra Cotta

Crochet Hook
- ☐ I-9 (5.5 mm) or size needed
  for gauge
- ☐ Yarn needle

SIZE INFORMATION
Size: 35" x 51" (89 cm x 129.5 cm)

GAUGE INFORMATION
One Hexagon = 7" / 18 cm from one flat side to opposite flat side

HEXAGON 1
Make 5
Round 1: With I, ch 4, 11 dc in 4th ch from hook, slip st to top of first ch-4 – 12 dc, (3 skipped chs count as dc). Fasten off.

Round 2: Join F in slip st, ch 3 (counts as dc now and throughout), dc in same space, ch 1, *2 dc in next st, ch 1; repeat from * 10 more times, slip st in top of first ch-3. Fasten off.

Round 3: Join E in any ch-1 space, ch 3, 2 dc in same ch-1 space, ch 2, *3 dc in next ch-1 space, ch 2; repeat from * 10 more times, ch 1, slip st in top of first ch-3. Fasten off.

Round 4: Join A in any ch-2 space, ch 3, 2 dc in same space, *ch 1, (3 dc, ch 2, 3 dc) in next ch-2 space, ch 1, 3 dc in next ch-2 space; repeat from * 4 more times, (3 dc, ch 2, 3 dc) in next ch-2 space, ch 1, slip st in top of first ch-3.

Round 5: Ch 3, turn, 2 dc in ch-2 space, ch 2, 3 dc in same space, *[ch 1, 3 dc in next ch-1 space] twice, ch 1, (3 dc, ch 2, 3 dc) in next ch-2 space; repeat from * 4 more times, [ch 1, 3 dc in next ch-1 space] twice, ch 1, slip st in top of first ch-3. Fasten off.

HEXAGON 2
Make 5
Work as for Hexagon 1, working Round 1 with H, Round 2 with D, Round 3 with G, and Rounds 4-5 with A.

HEXAGON 3
Make 5
Work as for Hexagon 1, working Round 1 with B, Round 2 with F, Round 3 with I, and Rounds 4-5 with A.

HEXAGON 4
Make 5

Work as for Hexagon 1, working
Round 1 with I, Round 2 with C,
Round 3 with H, and Rounds 4-5
with A.

HEXAGON 5
Make 5

Work as for Hexagon 1, working
Round 1 with H, Round 2 with F,
Round 3 with B, and Rounds 4-5
with A.

HEXAGON 6
Make 4

Work as for Hexagon 1, working
Round 1 with C, Round 2 with E,
Round 3 with H, and Rounds 4-5
with A.

HEXAGON 7
Make 4

Work as for Hexagon 1, working
Round 1 with G, Round 2 with D,
Round 3 with E, and Rounds 4-5
with A.

Assembly Diagram

HEXAGON 8
Make 4

Work as for Hexagon 1, working
Round 1 with G, Round 2 with C,
Round 3 with B, and Rounds 4-5
with A.

HEXAGON 9
Make 4

Work as for Hexagon 1, working Round 1 with E, Round 2 with D, Round 3 with I, and Rounds 4-5 with A.

HALF HEXAGON 10
Make 4

Row 1: With B, ch 4, 6 dc in 4th ch from hook – 7 dc, (3 skipped chs count as dc). Fasten off.
Row 2: Join F in first dc, ch 3, dc in same space, ch 1, *2 dc in next st, ch 1; repeat from * 5 more times. Fasten off.
Row 3: Join I in first dc, ch 4, *3 dc in next ch-1 space, ch 2; repeat from * 5 more times, ch 1, dc in last dc. Fasten off.
Row 4: Join A in first ch-1 space, ch 3, 2 dc in same space, *ch 1, 3 dc in next ch-2 space, (3 dc, ch 2, 3 dc) in next ch-2 space, ch 1; repeat from * once more, 3 dc in next ch-2 space, 3 dc in last ch-1 space.
Row 5: Ch 3, turn, 2 dc in first dc, *[ch 1, 3 dc in next ch-1 space] twice, ch 1, (3 dc, ch 2, 3 dc) in next ch-2 space; repeat from * once more, [ch 1, 3 dc in next ch-1 space] twice, ch 1, 3 dc in last dc. Fasten off.

HALF HEXAGON 11
Make 4

Work as for Half Hexagon 10, working Row 1 with G, Row 2 with D, Row 3 with E, and Rows 4-5 with A.

FINISHING

Following Assembly Diagram, arrange Hexagons into Afghan, 5 Full Hexagons wide by 9 Hexagons long. Whipstitch Hexagons together.

Edging

Round 1: With right side facing, join A in any st along outside edge, sc evenly spaced around all edges of Afghan, working 2 sc in each corner, slip st in first sc to join.
Round 2: Work reverse sc in each st around, slip st in first st. Fasten off.

Weave in ends.

Ripple Granny

Designed by Carrie Carpenter

 INTERMEDIATE

SHOPPING LIST

Yarn Worsted weight 4 yarn, 100% acrylic, [3 ½ oz /100g (approx 197 yds / 180m)]

- ☐ Color A: 3 Skeins Light Blue
- ☐ Color B: 2 Skeins Medium Blue
- ☐ Color C: 2 Skeins Dusty Pink
- ☐ Color D: 2 Skeins Medium Pink
- ☐ Color E: 2 Skeins Mauve
- ☐ Color F: 2 Skeins Medium Green
- ☐ Color G: 3 skins white

Crochet Hook

- ☐ H-8 (5 mm) or size needed for gauge
- ☐ Yarn needle

SIZE INFORMATION
Size: 42" x 66" (106.5 cm x 167.5 cm)

GAUGE INFORMATION
One Square = 6" / 15 cm

NOTES: Granny Squares are worked with right side facing throughout. Do not turn work at the ends of rounds or rows.
Granny Squares are joined together in corners on Joining Round to make a strip.
Ripple stitch pattern is worked across one edge of Granny Square Strip to make a Ripple Strip. Three Ripple Strips are made and are sewn together.

SPECIAL ABBREVIATIONS
Cluster: Keeping last loop of each dc on hook, work 3 dc into indicated ch-1 space and 3 dc in next ch-1 space, yo and draw through all loops on hook.

Joining Cluster: Keeping last loop of each dc on hook, work 3 dc into indicated ch-3 corner space of one Granny Square and 3 dc into ch-3 corner space of next Granny Square, yo and draw through all loops on hook.

RIPPLE STRIP 1
Granny Square 1
Make 6

With E, ch 5, join with slip st in first ch to form a ring.
Round 1: Ch 3 (counts as dc now and throughout), 2 dc in ring, [ch 3, 3 dc in ring] 3 times, ch 3, slip st to top of beginning ch to join. Fasten off.
Round 2: Join G with slip st in any ch-3 space, ch 3, (2 dc, ch 3, 3 dc) in same ch-3 space, *ch 1, (3 dc, ch 3, 3 dc) in next ch-3 space; repeat from * 2 more times, ch 1, slip st to top of beginning ch-3. Fasten off.
Round 3: Join B with slip st in any corner ch-3 space, ch 3, (2 dc, ch 3, 3 dc) in same ch-3 space, ch 1, 3 dc in next ch-1 space, ch 1, *(3 dc, ch 3, 3 dc) in next corner ch-3 space, ch 1,

3 dc in next ch-1 space; repeat from * 2 more times, ch 1, slip st to top of beginning ch-3. Fasten off.

Round 4: Join D with slip st in any corner ch-3 space, ch 3, (2 dc, ch 3, 3 dc) in same ch-3 space, ch 1, [3 dc in next ch-1 space, ch 1] twice, *(3 dc, ch 3, 3 dc) in next corner ch-3 space, ch 1, [3 dc in next ch-1 space, ch 1] twice; repeat from * 2 more times, slip st to top of beginning ch-3. Fasten off.

Granny Square Strip

Joining Round: Join G with slip st in any corner ch-3 space of First Granny Square, ch 3, (2 dc, ch 3, 3 dc) in same ch-3 space, *ch 1, [3 dc in next ch-1 space, ch 1] 3 times, (3 dc, ch 3, 3 dc) in next corner ch-3 space, ch 1, [3 dc in next ch-1 space, ch 1] 3 times, with right sides facing, hold corner of Second Granny Square next to corner of First Granny Square and work Joining Cluster; working along edge of Second Granny Square and leaving remaining edges of First Granny Square unworked, repeat from * to join six Granny Squares together along one long edge, working along remaining edges of Sixth Granny Square, [3 dc in next ch-1 space, ch 1] 3 times, (3 dc, ch 3, 3 dc) in next corner ch-3 space, ch 1, [3 dc in next ch-1 space, ch 1] 3 times, repeat

from * across opposite long edge of Granny Squares, [3 dc in next ch-1 space, ch 1] 3 times, (3 dc, ch 3, 3 dc) in next corner ch-3 space, ch 1, [3 dc in next ch-1 space, ch 1] 3 times, slip st to top of beginning ch-3. Fasten off.

Ripple Pattern

Row 1: With right side facing, join G with slip st in corner ch-3 space of First Granny Square, ch 3, *[3 dc in next ch-1 space, ch 1] 4 times, (3 dc, ch 3, 3 dc) in ch-3 space, [3 dc in next ch-1 space, ch 1] 3 times, work Cluster over next 2 ch-1 spaces; repeat from * to last Granny Square, ch 1, [3 dc in next ch-1 space, ch 1] 3 times, (3 dc, ch 3, 3 dc) in ch-3 space, ch 1, [3 dc in next ch-1 space, ch 1] 3 times, 3 dc in last ch-1 space, dc in last ch-3 space. Fasten off.

Row 2: Turn, change to A and repeat Row 1.

Row 3: Turn, change to B and repeat Row 1.

Row 4: Turn, change to A and repeat Row 1.

Row 5: Turn, change to F and repeat Row 1.

Row 6: Turn, change to G and repeat Row 1.

Row 7: Turn, change to C and repeat Row 1.

Row 8: Turn, change to D and repeat Row 1.

Row 9: Turn, change to E and repeat Row 1.

Row 10: Turn, change to D and repeat Row 1.

Row 11: Turn, change to C and repeat Row 1.

Row 12: Turn, change to G and repeat Row 1.

Row 13: Turn, change to F and repeat Row 1.

Row 14: Turn, change to A and repeat Row 1.

RIPPLE STRIP 2
Granny Square 2
Make 5

Work as for Granny Square 1, starting with D and working Round 1. Work Round 2 with B, Round 3 with F and Round 4 with A. Work Joining Round with G.

Half Granny Square
Make 2

With D, ch 5, join with slip st in first ch to form a ring.

Row 1: Ch 3, 2 dc in ring, ch 3, 3 dc in ring. Fasten off.

Row 2: Turn, join B with slip st in first dc, ch 3, 2 dc in same ch-3 space, ch 1, (3 dc, ch 3, 3 dc) in next ch-3 space, ch 1, 3 dc in last dc. Fasten off.

Row 3: Turn, join F with slip st in first dc, ch 3, 2 dc in same ch-3 space, ch 1, 3 dc in next ch-1 space, ch 1, (3 dc, ch 3, 3 dc) in next corner ch-3 space, ch 1, 3 dc in next ch-1 space, ch 1, 3 dc in last dc. Fasten off.

Row 4: Turn, join A with slip st in first dc, ch 3, 2 dc in same ch-3 space, ch 1, [3 dc in next ch-1 space, ch 1] twice, (3 dc, ch 3, 3 dc) in next corner ch-3 space, [ch 1, 3 dc in next ch-1 space, ch 1] 3 times. Fasten off.

Joining Round: Join G with slip st in first dc of of Half Granny Square, ch 3, 2 dc in same ch-3 space, *ch 1, [3 dc in next ch-1 space, ch 1] 3 times, (3 dc, ch 3, 3 dc) in next corner ch-3 space, ch 1, [3 dc in next ch-1 space, ch 1] 3 times, with right sides facing, hold corner of Second Granny Square next to corner of First Half Granny Square and work Joining Cluster; working along edge of Second Square and leaving remaining edges of First Square unworked, repeat from * to join five Granny Squares and last Half Granny Square together along one long edge, working along remaining edges of Half Granny Square, ch 3, 3 dc in next same space as last dc, [ch 1, 3 dc in next ch-1 space] 3 times, ch 1, (3 dc, ch 3, 3 dc) in first dc along opposite long edge, ch 1, [3 dc in next ch-1 space, ch 1] 3 times, repeat from * across opposite long edge of Granny Squares, [3 dc in next ch-1 space, ch 1] 3 times, (3 dc, ch 3, 3 dc) in last dc, ch 1, [3 dc in next ch-1 space, ch 1] 3 times along remaining edge of First Half Granny Square, slip st to top of beginning ch-3. Fasten off.

Ripple Pattern

Work Ripple Pattern as for Ripple Strip 1, working Row 1 with G, Row 2 with A, Row 3 with B, Row 4 with

A, Row 5 with F, Row 6 with G, Row 7 with C, Row 8 with D, Row 9 with E, Row 10 with D, Row 11 with C, Row 12 with G, Row 13 with F, Row 14 with A, Row 15 with B, Row 16 with E, Row 17 with A, and Row 18 with G.

RIPPLE STRIP 3
Granny Square

Work as for Granny Square 1, starting with E and working Round 1. Work Round 2 with A, Round 3 with C and Round 4 with B. Work Joining Round with G.

Ripple Pattern

Work Ripple Pattern as for Ripple Strip 1, working Row 1 with G, Row 2 with A, Row 3 with B, Row 4 with A, Row 5 with F, Row 6 with G, Row 7 with C, Row 8 with D, Row 9 with E, Row 10 with D, Row 11 with C, Row 12 with G, Row 13 with F, Row 14 with A, Row 15 with B, Row 16 with E, Row 17 with A, and Row 18 with G.

Second Ripple Pattern

Working along opposite edge of Granny Square Strip, work Ripple Pattern as for Ripple Strip 1, working Row 1 with G, Row 2 with A, Row 3 with E, Row 4 with B, Row 5 with A, Row 6 with F, Row 7 with G, Row 8 with C, Row 9 with D, Row 10 with E, Row 11 with D, Row 12 with C, Row 13 with G, Row 14 with F and Row 15 with A.

FINISHING

With G edges together, sew Ripple Strip 1 to Ripple Strip 2. Sew Ripple Strip 2 to Ripple Strip 3. Weave in all ends.

Colorful Hexagon

■■▢▷ **EASY**

SHOPPING LIST

Yarn Worsted weight
yarn, 100% acrylic, [3 ½ oz /100g
(approx 170 yds / 156m)]
- ☐ Color A: 3 Skeins Beige
- ☐ Color B: 2 Skeins Dusty Rose
- ☐ Color C: 2 Skeins Dusty Green
- ☐ Color D: 2 Skeins Mustard
- ☐ Color E: 2 Skeins Olive
- ☐ Color F: 2 Skeins Cranberry
- ☐ Color G: 2 Skeins Eggplant
- ☐ Color H: 2 Skeins Paprika

Crochet Hook
- ☐ I-9 (5.5 mm) or size needed
  for gauge
- ☐ Yarn needle

SIZE INFORMATION

Size: 45" x 60" (114.5 cm x 152.5 cm)

GAUGE INFORMATION

One Hexagon = 9" / 23 cm from one flat side to opposite flat side

HEXAGON B
Make 5

Round 1: With B, ch 4, dc in 4th ch from hook (3 skipped chs count as dc), work 11 dc same ch, slip st in top of beginning ch – 12 dc.

Round 2: Ch 5 (counts as dc and ch 2 now and throughout), dc in same space, dc in next dc, *(dc, ch 2, dc) in next dc, dc in next dc; repeat from * 4 more times, slip st in 3rd ch of beginning ch – 6 ch-2 spaces.

Round 3: Ch 3 (counts as dc now and throughout), dc in next dc, *(dc, ch 2, dc) in next ch-2 space, dc in next 3 dc; repeat from * 4 more times, (dc, ch 2, dc) in next ch-2 space, dc in last dc, slip st in top of beginning ch.

Round 4: Ch 3, dc in next 2 dc, *(dc, ch 2, dc) in next ch-2 space, dc in next 5 dc; repeat from * 4 more times, (dc, ch 2, dc) in next ch-2 space, dc in last 2 dc, slip st in top of beginning ch.

Round 5: Ch 3, dc in next 3 dc, *(dc, ch 2, dc) in next ch-2 space, dc in next 7 dc; repeat from * 4 more times, (dc, ch 2, dc) in next ch-2 space, dc in last 3 dc, slip st in top of beginning ch.

Round 6: Ch 3, dc in next 4 dc, *(dc, ch 2, dc) in next ch-2 space, dc in next 9 dc; repeat from * 4 more times, (dc, ch 2, dc) in next ch-2 space, dc in last 4 dc, slip st in top of beginning ch. Fasten off.

Round 7: Join A in any ch-2 space, ch 5, dc in same space, dc in next 11 dc, *(dc, ch 2, dc) in next ch-2 space, dc in next 11 dc; repeat from * 4 more times, slip st in 3rd ch of beginning ch. Fasten off.

HEXAGON C
Make 5

Work as for Hexagon B, working Rounds 1-6 with C and Round 7 with A.

HEXAGON D
Make 5
Work as for Hexagon B, working Rounds 1-6 with D and Round 7 with A.

HEXAGON E
Make 4
Work as for Hexagon B, working Rounds 1-6 with E and Round 7 with A.

HEXAGON F
Make 4
Work as for Hexagon B, working Rounds 1-6 with F and Round 7 with A.

HEXAGON G
Make 4
Work as for Hexagon B, working Rounds 1-6 with G and Round 7 with A.

HEXAGON H
Make 4
Work as for Hexagon B, working Rounds 1-6 with H and Round 7 with A.

Assembly Diagram

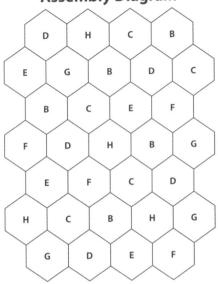

FINISHING
Following Assembly Diagram, arrange Hexagons into Afghan, 5 Hexagons at widest point by 7 Hexagons long. Whipstitch Hexagons together.

Edging
Round 1: With right side facing, join A in any st along outside edge, hdc evenly spaced around all edges of Afghan, working 2 hdc in each ch-2 space, slip st in first sc to join.

Weave in ends.

Red, White & Turquoise

 **EASY**

SHOPPING LIST

Yarn Worsted weight
yarn, 100% acrylic, [7oz /198g
(approx 364yds /333m)]
- ☐ Color A: 1 Skein Burgundy
- ☐ Color B: 3 skeins Soft White
- ☐ Color C: 2 Skeins Turquoise

Crochet Hook
- ☐ I-9 (5.5 mm) or size needed
  for gauge
- ☐ Yarn needle

SIZE INFORMATION

Size: 45" x 53" (114.5 cm x 134.5 cm)

GAUGE INFORMATION

One Square = 8" / 20.5 cm

GRANNY SQUARE
Make 30

Round 1: With A, ch 4, dc in 4th ch from hook (3 skipped chs count as dc), dc in same ch, [ch 3, 3 dc in same ch] 3 times, ch 3, slip st in top of beginning ch – 12 dc and 4 ch-3 spaces.

Round 2: Turn, slip st to first ch-3 space, ch 3 (counts as dc now and throughout), (2 dc ch 3, 3 dc) in same ch-3 space, *skip next dc, dc in center dc, skip next dc, (3 dc ch 3, 3 dc) in ch-3 space; repeat from * 2 more times, skip next dc, dc in center dc, skip next dc, slip st to top of beginning ch to join. Fasten off.

Round 3: Turn, join B in any center dc, ch 3, 2 dc in same st, ch 1, *(3 dc, ch 3, 3 dc) in next ch-3 space, ch 1, 3 dc in next dc, ch 1; repeat from * 2 more times, (3 dc, ch 3, 3 dc) in next ch-3 space, ch 1, slip st to top of beginning ch-3.

Round 4: Turn, slip st to next ch-1 space, ch 3, 2 dc in same ch-1 space, ch 1, *(3 dc, ch 3, 3 dc) in next ch-3 space, [ch 1, 3 dc in next ch-1 space] twice, ch 1; repeat from * 2 more times, (3 dc, ch 3, 3 dc) in next ch-3 space, ch 1, 3 dc in next ch-1 space, ch 1, slip st to top of beginning ch-3.

Round 5: Turn, slip st to next ch-1 space, ch 3, 2 dc in same ch-1 space, ch 1, *(3 dc, ch 3, 3 dc) in next ch-3 space, [ch 1, 3 dc in next ch-1 space] 3 times, ch 1; repeat from * 2 more times, (3 dc, ch 3, 3 dc) in next ch-3 space, [ch 1, 3 dc in next ch-1 space] twice, ch 1, slip st to top of beginning ch-3. Fasten off.

Round 6: Turn, join C in any st, sc in each dc and ch around, working 2 sc in each corner ch, slip st to first sc. Fasten off.

FINISHING

Arrange Squares into Afghan, 5
Squares wide x 6 Squares long.
Whipstitch Hexagons together.

Edging

Round 1: With right side facing, join
C in any st along outside edge, dc
evenly spaced around all edges of
Afghan, working 3 dc in each corner,
slip st in top of beginning ch to join.

Round 2: Ch 3, turn, *dc in next
dc, ch 1, skip next dc; repeat from
* around, working 3 dc in center
dc in each corner, slip st in top of
beginning ch.

Round 3: Ch 3, turn, *dc in next ch-1
space, ch 1; repeat from * around,
working 3 dc in center dc in each
corner, slip st in top of beginning ch.

Round 4: Ch 4, turn, (dc, ch 1, tr, ch
1, dc, ch 1, dc) all in same dc, *skip
2 dc and 2 ch-1 spaces, (dc, ch 1, dc,
ch 1, tr, ch 1, dc, ch 1, dc) all in next
dc; repeat from * around, slip st in
3rd ch of beginning ch. Fasten off.

Weave in ends.

Off Center Granny Square

 **EASY**

SHOPPING LIST

Yarn Worsted weight
yarn, 100% acrylic, [7oz /198g
(approx 364yds /333m)]
- ☐ Color A: 2 Skeins Navy
- ☐ Color B: 2 Skeins Medium Blue
- ☐ Color C: 2 Skeins Aran
- ☐ Color D: 2 Skeins Medium green

Crochet Hook

I-9 (5.5 mm) or size needed
for gauge
needle

SIZE INFORMATION

Size: 35" x 42" (89 cm x 106.5 cm)

GAUGE INFORMATION

One Square = 7" / 18 cm

GRANNY SQUARE 1

Make 15

Row 1: With D, ch 4, 2 dc in 4th ch from hook, [ch 3, 3 dc] 3 times, ch 3, slip st to top of first ch-4 to join.

Row 2: Ch 3 (counts as dc now and throughout), turn, 2 dc in ch-3 space, ch 3, 3 dc in same space, *ch 1, (3 dc, ch 3, 3 dc) in next ch-3 space; repeat from * 2 more times, ch 1, slip st to top of first ch-3. Fasten off

Row 3: Turn, join C in one corner ch-3 space, ch 3, 2 dc in same space, ch 1, 3 dc in next ch-1 space, ch 1, (3 dc, ch 3, 3 dc) in next corner ch-3 space, ch 1, 3 dc in next ch-1 space, ch 1, 3 dc in next corner ch-3 space.

Row 4: Ch 4 (counts as dc and ch 1 now and throughout), turn, [3 dc in next ch-1 space, ch 1] twice, (3 dc, ch 3, 3 dc) in next corner ch-3 space, [ch 1, 3 dc in next ch-1 space] twice, ch 1, dc in last dc. Fasten off.

Row 5: Turn, join B in first ch-1 space, ch 3, 2 dc in same space, [ch 1, 3 dc in next ch-1 space] twice, ch 1, (3 dc, ch 3, 3 dc) in corner ch-3 space, [ch 1, 3 dc in next ch-1 space] 3 times.

Row 6: Ch 4, turn, [3 dc in next ch-1 space, ch 1] 3 times, (3 dc, ch 3, 3 dc) in corner ch-3 space, [ch 1, 3 dc in next ch-1 space] 3 times, ch 1, dc in last dc. Fasten off.

Row 7: Turn, join C in first ch-1 space, ch 3, 2 dc in same space, [ch 1, 3 dc in next ch-1 space] 3 times, ch 1, (3 dc, ch 3, 3 dc) in corner ch-3 space, [ch 1, 3 dc in next ch-1 space] 4 times.

Row 8: Ch 4, turn, [3 dc in next ch-1 space, ch 1] 4 times, (3 dc, ch 3, 3 dc) in next corner ch-3 space, [ch 1, 3 dc in next ch- space] 4 times, ch 1, dc in last dc. Fasten off.

Note: Rounds 9-10 will be worked in rounds around all edges of Granny Square.

Round 9: Join A in any corner ch-3 space, ch 3, 2 dc in same space, ch 3, 3 dc in same space, *[ch 1, 3 dc in next ch-1 space] 4 times, (3 dc, ch 3, 3 dc) in corner ch-3 space; repeat from * twice more, [ch 1, 3 dc in next ch-1 space] 4 times, ch 1, slip st to top of first ch-3.

Round 10: Slip st to corner ch-3 space, ch 3, 2 dc in same space, ch 3, 3 dc in same space, *[ch 1, 3 dc in next ch-1 space] 5 times, (3 dc, ch 3, 3 dc) in corner ch-3 space; repeat from * twice more, [ch 1, 3 dc in next ch-1 space] 5 times, ch 1, slip st to top of first ch-3.
Fasten off.

GRANNY SQUARE 2
Make 15

Work as for Granny Square 1, working Row 1-2 with B, Rows 3-4 with C, Rows 5-6 with D, Rows 7-8 with C and Rounds 9-10 with A.

Assembly Diagram

2	1	2	1	2
1	2	1	2	1
2	1	2	1	2
1	2	1	2	1
2	1	2	1	2
1	2	1	2	1

FINISHING

Following Assembly Diagram, arrange Granny Squares into Afghan, 5 squares wide by 6 Squares long. Whipstitch Squares together. Weave in ends.

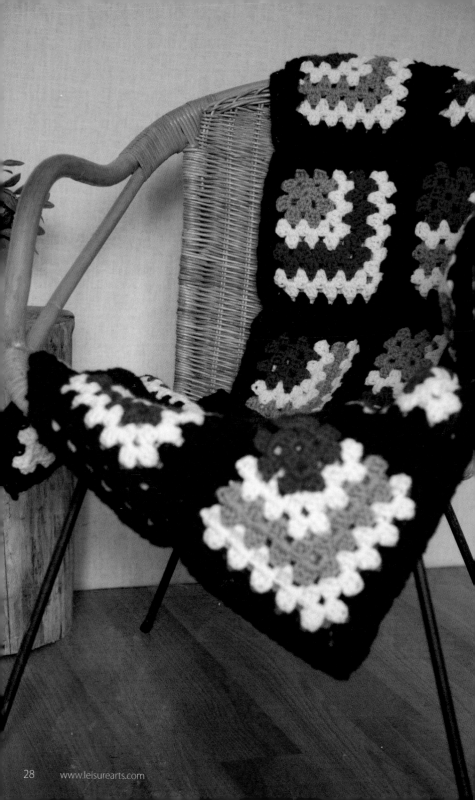

General Instructions

ABBREVIATIONS

approx	approximately
ch	chain
cm	centimeter(s)
dc	double crochet
dc2tog	double crochet 2 stitches together
g	gram(s)
hdc	half double crochet
m	meter(s)
mm	millimeters
oz	ounce(s)
RS	right side
sc	single crochet
sc2tog	single crochet 2 stitches together
sk	skip
sl st	slip stitch
sp(s)	space(s)
st(s)	stitch(es)
tr	treble crochet
WS	wrong side
yd(s)	yard(s)

CROCHET HOOKS															
U.S.	B-1	C-2	D-3	E-4	F-5	G-6	H-8	I-9	J-10	K-10½	L-11	M/N-13	N/P-15	P/Q	Q	S
Metric - mm	2.25	2.75	3.25	3.5	3.75	4	5	5.5	6	6.5	8	9	10	15	16	19

SKILL LEVELS

◼☐☐☐ **BEGINNER**	Projects for first-time crocheters using basic stitches. Minimal shaping.
◼◼☐☐ **EASY**	Projects using yarn with basic stitches, repetitive stitch patterns, simple color changes, and simple shaping and finishing.
◼◼◼☐ **INTERMEDIATE**	Projects using a variety of techniques, such as basic lace patterns or color patterns, mid-level shaping and finishing.
◼◼◼◼ **EXPERIENCED**	Projects with intricate stitch patterns, techniques and dimension, such as non-repeating patterns, multi-color techniques, fine threads, small hooks, detailed shaping and refined finishing.

YARN WEIGHTS

Yarn Weight Symbol & Names	LACE 0	SUPER FINE 1	FINE 2	LIGHT 3	MEDIUM 4	BULKY 5	SUPER BULKY 6
Type of Yarns in Category	Fingering, 10-count crochet thread	Sock, Fingering Baby	Sport, Baby	DK, Light Worsted	Worsted, Afghan, Aran	Chunky, Craft, Rug	Bulky, Roving
Crochet Gauge* Ranges in Single Crochet to 4" (10 cm)	32-42 double crochets**	21-32 sts	16-20 sts	12-17 sts	11-14 sts	8-11 sts	5-9 sts
Advised Hook Size Range	Steel*** 6,7,8 Regular hook B-1	B-1 to E-4	E-4 to 7	7 to I-9	I-9 to K-10.5	K-10.5 to M-13	M-13 and larger

*GUIDELINES ONLY: The chart above reflects the most commonly used gauges and hook sizes for specific yarn categories.

** Lace weight yarns are usually crocheted on larger-size hooks to create lacy openwork patterns. Accordingly, a gauge range is difficult to determine. Always follow the gauge stated in your pattern.

*** Steel crochet hooks are sized differently from regular hooks–the higher the number the smaller the hook, which is the reverse of regular hook sizing.

Yarn Information

For your convenience, listed below are the yarns
used to create our photography models.

Sunburst Hexagon
Vanna's Choice by Lion Brand
Color A: 5 Skeins White #100
Color B: 1 Skein Eggplant #142
Color C: 1 Skein Dusty Rose #140
Color D: 1 Skein Silver Blue #105
Color E: 1 Skein Rose #142
Color F: 1 Skein Dusty Green #173
Color G: 1 Skein Fern #171
Color H: 1 Skein Aqua #102
Color I: 1 Skein Terra Cotta #134

Granny Ripple
Waverly For Bernat
Color A: 3 Skeins Breath of Blue
#55148
Color B: 2 Skeins Blue Gown #55145
Color C: 2 Skeins Princess #55415
Color D: 2 Skeins Fresh Flower
#55401
Color E: 2 Skeins Mauve Glow
#55402
Color F: 2 Skeins Celadon #55280
Color G: 3 Skeins Cream Puff #55007

Fall Colors Hexagon
Vanna's Choice by Lion Brand
Color A: 3 Skeins Beige #123
Color B: 2 Skeins Dusty rose #142
Color C: 2 Skeins Dusty green #173
Color D: 2 Skeins mustard #158
Color E: 2 Skeins olive #174
Color F: 2 Skeins cranberry #180
Color G: 2 Skeins eggplant #145
Color H: 2 Skeins terra cotta #134

Red, White and Turquoise
Red Heart Super Saver Economy
Color A: 1 Skein Burgundy #376
Color B: 3 Skeins Soft White #316
Color C: 2 Skeins Turquoise #512

Off Center Granny
Red Heart Super Saver Economy
Color A: 2 Skeins Soft Navy #0387
Color B: 2 Skeins Blue Suede #3945
Color C: 2 Skeins Aran #0313
Color D: 2 Skeins Paddy Green
#0368

We have made every effort to ensure that these instructions are accurate and complete. We cannot, however, be responsible for human error, typographical mistakes, or variations in individual work.

Production Team: Produced for Leisure Arts, Inc. by Candice Jensen Productions – Editor: Heather Vantress – Layout: Rita Sowins – Technical editing: Peggy Greig – Photography by: Silvana Di Franco